M000098344

This Notebook Belongs To

____

Made in the USA
Monee, IL
27 November 2020

49712963R10069